foreword

In preparation for designing this book, we visited several fabric stores. We were surprised at the number of teens we saw in the fleece department. As an experiment we decided to recruit our own team of teenagers to see what type of prints they would select and how they would construct their own throws.

Our teenage "apprentices" were amazed and overwhelmed with the choice of fleece available. "So much fleece, so little time," they said. But they persevered, made their purchases and headed home to make their throws. While chatting, laughing and, of course, eating—they worked on their projects. See their creations on pages 4, 6 and 8. We think they did a fantastic job.

Now we had to come up with 17 other throws to complete this book. We could maybe come up with four or five no-sew designs. But 17! No Way!! Once we got started though, this became more of a challenge than an impossibility. We got our scissors and irons going—snipped, cut, fringed, tied and pressed—and we think we have come up with some very unique and clever no-sew fleece throws. See if you agree.

There's a wide variety of choices on the following pages—from elegant, to funky, to cute. Now it's your turn. See what original designs you can come up with by just putting different color combinations and prints together. You'll see how easy and fun it is to make your own no-sew throw.

table of contents

fleece facts

Please familiarize yourself with the following facts and instructions before beginning the projects in this book:

• Fleece is usually 60" wide. It's important to cut off the selvage edges before measuring the fleece for your throw.

• To determine the right and wrong side of the fleece, stretch the fabric along the cut edge of the fleece. The fleece will curl to the wrong side. Mark your cut piece with a marking pencil before you start your project.

• Fusing: Most of the projects in this book were constructed by using fusing products. We particularly liked Steam-A-Seam 2® by Warm Company and used it for both adding appliques and joining two pieces of fabric together. This two-sided fusible adhesive is available in various widths—from ¼" to 24" either in packages or by the yard.

This product makes no-sew projects easier than ever. A pressure-sensitive coating on both sides of the web allows it to temporarily stick to the applique material, then adheres the applique piece to the background. The applique stays in place without shifting and is repositionable until pressed with an iron. After you're satisfied with your design, you can use a pressing cloth and iron the applique on. For best results, follow the manufacturer's instructions before using fusible products.

• Tracing the patterns: Place tracing paper over the pattern and trace pattern. Cut out pattern along drawn lines. Pin the pattern to the fleece and cut out.

• Marking fleece: A Chacopel pencil is great for marking. It's available in either light or dark chalk so that it can be used on any color of fleece. After marking, you can use the brush on the end of the pencil to erase your marks.

• Fabric care: Fleece doesn't shrink, so there's no need for pre-washing.
For laundering, use a powdered laundry detergent and luke warm water on a gentle cycle. Liquid fabric softeners shouldn't be used.
For drying, place in the dryer with no dryer sheets and dry on low for a short time.
For ironing, use steam and a pressing cloth. Never touch the iron directly to the fleece.

• Hemming edges or lining fleece is optional. This depends on your own personal preference.

• Curling fringe: Some fleece fabrics curl really well and others don't. Before you purchase your fleece, test a small piece. Your fabric store clerk will let you try a small sample. Cut a strip ½" wide across the crosswise grain then stretch it and see if and how much it will curl.
To curl the fleece for your finished project, hold onto one end of the fringe and pull the other end tightly. (Example of curled fringe on page 20)

General Supplies

Measuring tape	Yard stick
Fabric marker	Chacopel pencil
Pins	Tracing paper
Iron	Pressing cloth
Pencil	Scissors or rotary cutter

Seen below and on the next two pages are the traditional cut-and-fringed throws that were made by our teenage "apprentices". This type of throw is easy, quick and fun to make and a great project for someone wanting to try a no-sew throw. The basic instructions for the cut-and-fringed throw are at right. After you've mastered this technique, try your hand at some of the others in this book.

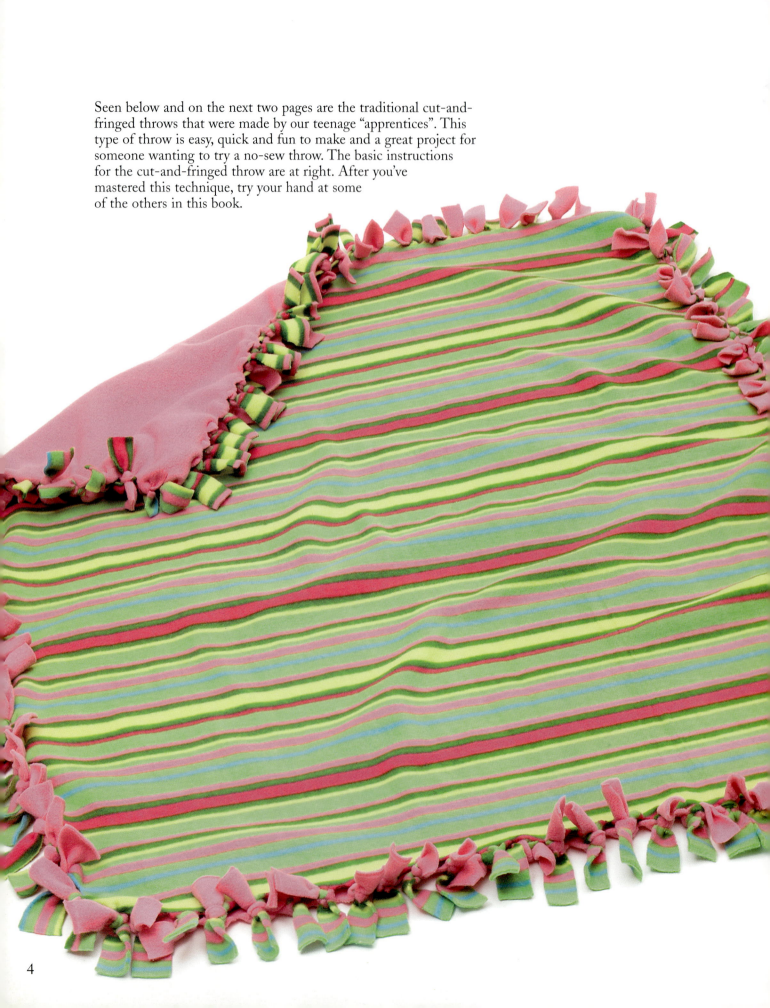

Our three happy shoppers have made their final selections. Loren, Kelly and Dana are now ready to go home and start creating their throws.

spring fling

Kelly chose this particular print because her room is decorated in the same shades of pinks and greens and also because she's partial to stripes. She wanted a throw that she could keep in her room but also take along to football games. She's looking forward to wrapping up in her throw while cheering her team on to victory.

You'll need:
Fleece:
  1½ yds. striped
  1½ yds. pink

Finished size: 52" x 58"

1. Cut both the striped and pink fleece 52" x 58".

2. With wrong sides together, lay both pieces of fleece on a flat surface matching edges. Pin the pieces around the edges to secure.

3. Cut 1" x 4" fringe all around the throw, through both thicknesses.

4. Tie the striped and pink fringe together using a double knot.

make a wish

Maybe you don't have a telescope to peer at the stars, but the heavens can be found right in your own room when you sleep under this celestial cover-up. Dana created this delightful throw, choosing the star print fabric to coordinate with the reds and blues of her bedspread. She plans to take it along to her next sleepover to impress her friends and maybe even teach them how to make their own throw.

You'll need:
Fleece:
  2 yds. star print
  2 yds. red
Chacopel pencil

Finished size: 58" x 70"

1. Cut both print and red fleece 58" x 70".

2. Fold each piece into fourths. Using a Chacopel pencil, draw a curved line between two of the corners. See diagram at right (A). Cut along the line. Repeat on the second piece of fleece.

3. Open up both pieces, and with wrong sides facing, lay on a flat surface with the edges matching. Pin around the edges to secure.

4. Cut 1½" x 4" fringe around the throw, through both thicknesses.

5. Tie the star fleece and the red backing fringe together using a double knot.

A

fold

fold

Here's an example of real teamwork in action. Dana works on one side of the throw while Kelly works on the other. They'll be finished with this project in no time.

Dana is busily tying the fringe around her celestial-inspired throw.

bon voyage

What a bright and funky print Kelly selected to make this fun and colorful throw. The theme is travel and the print displays images of travel stickers, post cards, stamps and suitcases. Is she planning to take this throw on her next road trip? Or will it just find a place in her room displayed on her bed? She can look at it and dream of the many places she'd like to see.

You'll need:
Fleece:
  2 yds. print
  2 yds. blue

Finished size: 58" x 70"

1. Cut the print and the blue fleece 58" x 70".

2. With wrong sides together, lay both pieces of fleece on a flat surface matching edges. Pin around the edges to secure.

3. Cut 1½" x 4" fringe around the throw through both thicknesses.

4. Tie the print and blue fringe together.

loop de loop

The stripes in this throw range from the frothy green of the sea to the deep blue of a reflective pool. Add to this the misty purple and you have a sleek and elegant afghan. It's just the accessory to throw over an Adirondack chair on the porch of a beach cottage. This cover-up is so easy to make, you'll want to make several. Fringe is cut on each edge and then tied to form decorative loops.

Instructions on page 44

glowing wild

Plaid goes wild. Every bright color is represented in this fun and fancy throw ideal for a teen's room. Squares of purple, blue, lime green, turquoise and deep magenta seem to pop from this wild print. She'll love the fringed edges embellished with matching foam beads. Look closely—you'll see that each bead threaded on the fringe represents a distinctive shape—squares, hearts and circles—all in the same bright colors displayed in the fleece. The beads are threaded onto the fringe using a large plastic needle. How clever is that?

Instructions on page 45

stadium seating

Here's the ideal accessory to take along to the big game. The handy pouch contains a full size throw…soft enough to sit on and warm enough to cover up when the weather gets chilly. The construction is so easy—even your kids could make this one—maybe for their dad's next birthday. A rectangle of fabric is simply fringed then tied together to form the pouch. The football is ironed onto the flap, then a strip of Velcro is added for closing. The throw is cut and fringed around the edge and ready to accompany your favorite sports fan to the next game.

Instructions page 46

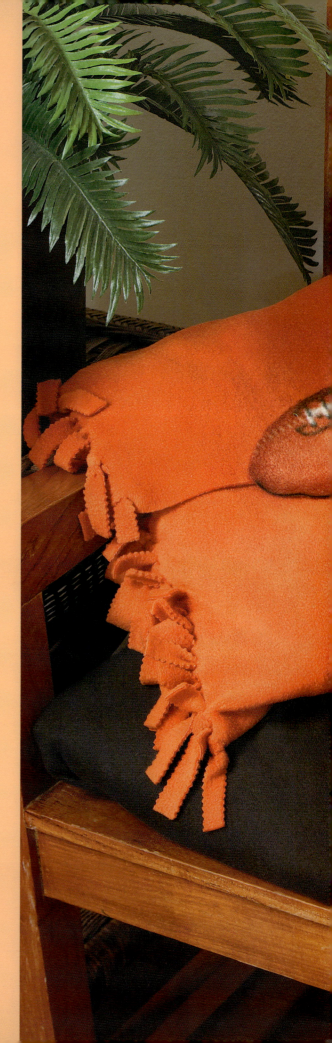

it's a sporting life

Whether you're taking this to the next ball game or just helping to decorate a sports fan's room, this throw is certain to please the youngster of the house. Is he or she a Little Leaguer? If so, they'll be thrilled with the images of baseballs, mitts and bats sprinkled throughout this sporty design. The bright royal blue contrasts nicely with the basic black squares and the sports-themed print. Batter Up!

Instructions on page 47

fly away home

What little girl doesn't love ladybugs? Here's the throw of her dreams. A trio of ladybugs surrounds a ground of black, giving this cover-up a very stylish, graphic design. The white top is backed with red fleece, then tied together for a colorful fringe. Ladybugs are the design of choice for so many young girls. Your's will be happy to help you with some of the tasks involved, such as cutting the circles or the fringe. Then she'll be able to claim ownership of her very own design.

Instructions on page 48

perfect petals

Your daughter will greet each day with a smile when she sees this pretty throw decorating her room. The bright pink petals accented with glowing orange, feature curly fleece centers that add just a touch of whimsy. The pretty rosettes are combined with a flashy plaid fabric that coordinates perfectly with the vivid shades of magenta and orange. The edges of this no-sew throw are pinked and rounded for a bit of style.

Preparing a work surface for fusing

Prepare an ironing surface on a large table or on the floor for projects which require fusing but are too large to easily handle on an ironing board. To do this, lay a blanket or comforter on the desired work surface, then cover the comforter with muslin or scrap cotton fabric.

Use a piece of muslin or scrap cotton fabric to protect your ironing board from stray fusible adhesives.

Pressing fleece

When working with fleece, you should always use a pressing cloth. It is not recommended to iron directly on the fleece. Direct contact can leave a permanent imprint.

It is helpful to keep iron cleaner handy for occasional accidents.

Instructions on page 49

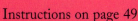

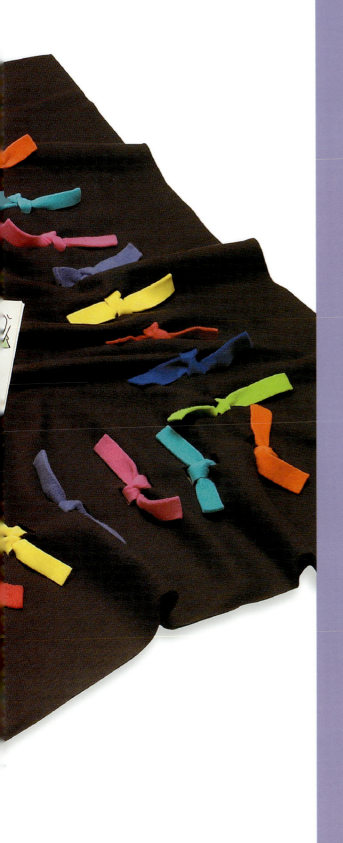

it's a tie

Don't throw away your scraps of fleece. You can use little bits of brightly colored scraps to create this clever throw. Each color of fleece is cut into strips, then tied to pre-cut slits in the navy fleece. This one includes bright primary colors, but you might choose to use print scraps for a completely different effect. Pastel shades would be charming on a background of pale pink or blue. Whatever combination you decide to use, you can be sure your throw will be a one-of-a-kind creation.

Instructions on page 50

starry, starry night

Need a baby shower gift in a hurry? You can literally make this fleece coverlet in one evening. Then take it to the shower and wow the group with this delightful throw embellished with a shower of stars. The center square is ironed onto the pastel plaid, then the cut-out stars border the throw for a heavenly effect. Yarn ties decorate the star cut-outs and add a little texture and dimension. The outside edge is fringed and then you're finished. Wasn't that easy?

Instructions on page 51

Fusing

To use any fusible product, follow the manufacturer's instructions carefully, otherwise an insufficient bond may result.

Always test the fusible product you are using on a piece of scrap fabric before making the project, testing the bond and adjusting conditions as recommended by the manufacturer.

We used Steam-A-Seam2® fusible web for most of the projects in this book. We loved it because it was repositionable. See instructions below for fusing appliqués:

1. Trace appliqué design on the paper liner and remove the second liner. Check to see which liner removes first by peeling apart at the corner.

2. Stick the fusible web to the wrong side of the fleece.

3. Cut the fusible web and fleece together along the traced lines.

4. Peel off remaining paper liner (leaving the web on the fleece) and stick the appliqué to the second piece of fleece. Reposition as desired.

5. Press for 10 – 15 seconds using a pressing cloth. Move iron around over the fleece so that it doesn't leave an imprint on the fabric. Adjust temperature and fusing time to the fleece. Check to see if the fabric has bonded. If not, press again.

over the rainbow

Your little munchkin will love this rainbow throw. The patchwork squares are cut and arranged this way and that for optimum effect. The narrow ties decorate each square resembling an authentic tied quilt. But this one is much easier to make. The squares are ironed on and the edge is fringed. That's it! And the pretty pastel shades will fit perfectly in the baby's nursery.

Instructions on page 52

diamonds are forever

Beautiful pastel diamonds border this soft, luscious fleece throw. Designed to coordinate with the muted shades of shabby chic decorating, this feminine throw would please any flea market shopper. Tossed casually on a bed or folded over a sofa, it's the perfect accessory for a vintage décor. To complete the faux-quilted look, the edges are trimmed to evoke the prairie points of a classical quilt design.

Instructions on page 53

dutch treat

Created to resemble Delft tiles, this throw would fit nicely with any blue-decorated room. The "tiles" are actually created using a foam stamp and acrylic paint. Then the squares are trimmed using a rotary cutter with a wavy edge blade. The edge of the blue fabric is also cut with a scalloped edge. The result—a throw that is reminiscent of traditional dutch design.

Instructions on page 54

sleeping beauty

This inviting throw just seems to say, "C'mon, take a nap." You're deserving of a peaceful respite from the day's pressures. Your own special retreat is only a dream away as you snuggle up in this comfy sage green throw. The edges are uniquely laced with a pale green fleece strip to lend a look of casual elegance. Grab a book, have a sip of tea and just feel your worries vanish into thin air.

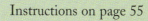

Instructions on page 55

windows

The cool shades of jewel tones accent this classy afghan. The surprise is in the cut-and-fold squares. So easy. The folds are tacked slightly to give a touch of dimension to the throw. Showing through the opening of each square is the classic black background. Just think how many different effects you can achieve merely by changing the colors of this afghan. Try experimenting and see what you can come up with.

Instructions on page 56

tranquility

Crisp, classic lines are set off by just a hint of black peeking between the folds. Asian accents include the Chinese frogs artfully closing this throw. The understated simplicity is a prime example of an Asian-inspired accessory. The look is soft and subdued and completely natural. Thrown over a bed or a sofa, this afghan can instantly change the ambience in a room and create a space that radiates serenity and comfort.

Instructions on page 57

cut to be tied

If your style tends toward traditional classic design, you'll love this elegant throw. It imitates the drawnwork technique so traditional in antique linens. The throw is composed of many tiny slits which are tied together with narrow fleece strips for a lacy, artistic effect. The dreamy sea foam green is layered atop a pale lavender which barely peeks through the cutwork border. This subtle use of color is an appealing addition to the clever construction of the throw.

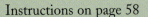

Instructions on page 58

primary colors

This eye-popping throw is garnished to perfection with neon bright stripes. The black fleece is cut into an afghan sized piece, then cut with little slits. Now here's the fun part— the brightly colored strips are woven in and out of the pre-cut slits to give the illusion of colorful confetti. Now drape this masterpiece over your sofa and wait for the compliments.

Instructions on page 59

dream weaver

Over and under you go—weaving strips of apple green and turquoise fleece to create this original design. The backing is a sophisticated pink which contrasts beautifully with this mix of interesting colors. This afghan resembles a patchwork quilt. But guess what? You don't have to sew a stitch. You don't even have to join a quilting bee. All you have to do to create this original creation is cut, weave and fringe. It might not win a blue ribbon in the county fair's quilting contest, but it will certainly be a prize winner around your house.

Instructions on page 60

loop de loop

(page 10)

You'll need:

Fleece:
  2 yds. green/blue/purple stripe

Finished size: 44" x 54"

1. Cut fleece 44" x 70".

2. Turn the edge of one short side up 8" and pin along the top edge. See diagram below.

3. Cut ½" x 4" strips along the folded edge.

4. Tie the strips in knots to form loops (A).

5. Repeat with the opposite end.

A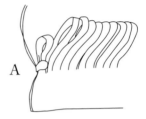

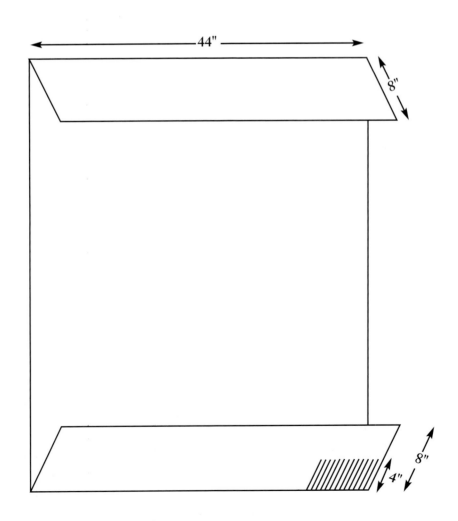

glowing wild

(page 12)

You'll need:
1¾ yds. brightly colored plaid fleece
Colorful foam beads, asst. shapes
Large plastic needle

Finished size: 55" x 58"

1. Cut fleece 55" x 58".

2. Cut ½" x 4" fringe on the two short ends of the throw.

3. Use a large plastic needle to attach the foam beads to every fifth fringe. Thread the beads at various lengths for interest. Tie a knot right under the bead to secure.

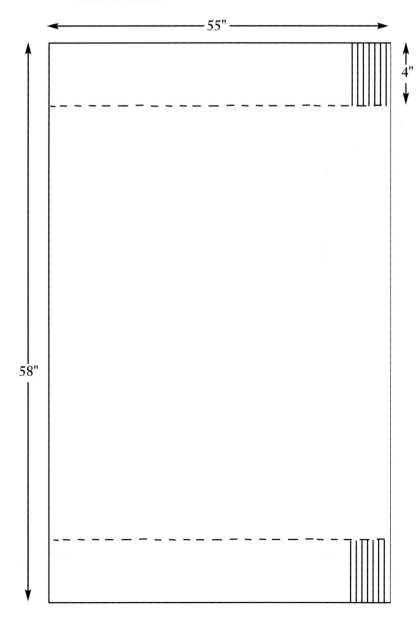

stadium seating

(page 14)

You'll need:
Fleece:
  1 yd. burnt orange
  1½ yds. football print
½ yd. Steam-A-Seam 2®, 18" wide
Pinking shears
Velcro strip
Pressing cloth

1. For the pouch: Cut orange fleece 24" x 42". Cut ½" x 3" fringe on the two long edges using pinking shears.

2. Mark 6" down from the top edge of the pouch. Fold the bottom 36" length in half. Tie the fringe on each folded edge up to the 6" mark. Refer to diagram.

3. To finish the pouch: Tie every two strips together of the side fringe on the 6" top portion for decoration only.

4. Cut a football image from the print fabric. Cut a piece of Steam-A-Seam 2® to cover one half of the football shape and apply it to the top half of the football (see photo at left). Peel off the backing paper and use a pressing cloth to iron this piece to the flap of the pouch as pictured.

5. Sew the strips of Velcro to the back of the bottom edge of the football and the front of the pouch for closing.

6. For the throw: Cut the football print fleece 48" x 60". Fringe the edges of the throw if desired. Insert in the pouch.

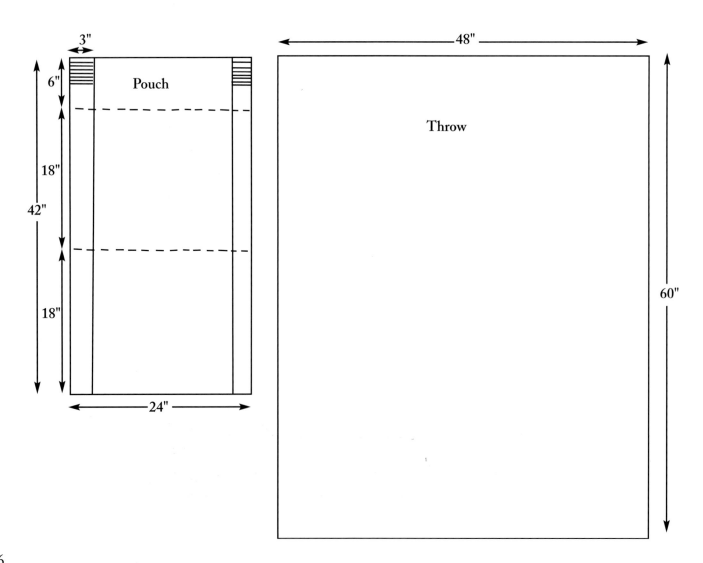

it's a sporting life

(page 16)

You'll need:
Fleece:
 1¾ yds. royal blue
 ¾ yd. black
 ½ yd. baseball print
Gold colored embroidery floss
Steam-A-Seam 2® fusing
 tape, ½" wide
Tapestry needle

Finished size 44" x 60"

1. Cut the blue fleece 44" x 60".

2. Cut six 12" black squares.

3. Cut six 8½" squares of the baseball print fabric.

4. Use a blanket stitch and 6 strands of embroidery floss to sew the baseball squares on the black squares as in the diagram.

5. Apply fusing tape to the black squares. Peel off the backing paper and use a pressing cloth to iron them to the blue fleece according to the diagram.

6. Cut a ¼" x 3" fringe all around the throw.

Option: As an alternative to the blanket stitch, iron the baseball squares to the black squares using the fusing tape.

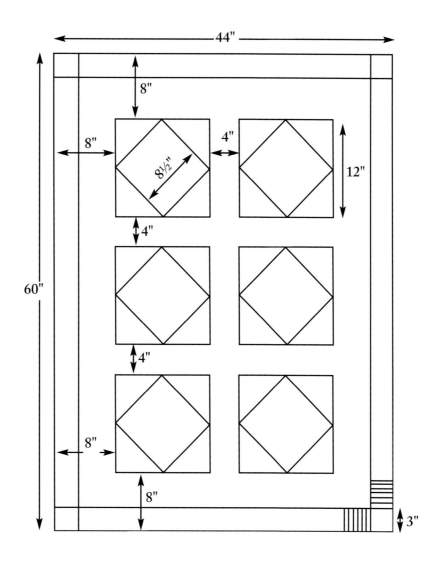

fly away home

(page 18)

You'll need:
Fleece:
  2 yds. red
  1⅓ yds. white
  1 yd. black
1½ yds. Steam-A-Seam 2®
  fusing tape, ½" wide
3 yds. Steam-A-Seam 2®, 18" wide
Pressing cloth

Finished size: 45" x 54"

1. Cut a piece of white and a piece of red 45" x 54". Cut a piece of black fleece 21" x 30".

2. To make the dots for the ladybugs: Cut a strip of black fleece 3" x 50". Apply a strip of 3" x 50" Steam-A-Seam 2® to the black strip. Trace eighteen 2½" circles (pattern on page 63) onto the paper side of Steam-A-Seam 2® then cut them out and set aside.

3. To make the ladybugs: Cut three 13" squares of red. Apply 13" squares of Steam-A-Seam 2® to the red squares. Make a paper pattern using the pattern on page 63 and trace to the paper side of Steam-A-Seam 2®. Cut out three red circles. Cut the red circles in half.

4. Peel off the backing paper and use a pressing cloth to iron the black circles to the red half circles.

5. To assemble the throw: Apply fusing tape to the edges of the 21" x 30" piece of black fleece. Peel off the backing paper, turn over and center on the white piece, then iron on.

6. Peel the backing paper off the ladybug pieces and iron to the throw following the diagram below.

7. Place the white fleece on the red backing fleece with wrong sides together and edges matching. Pin, then cut ¼" x 4" fringe all around the edges of the throw.

8. Tie the white and red fringe together.

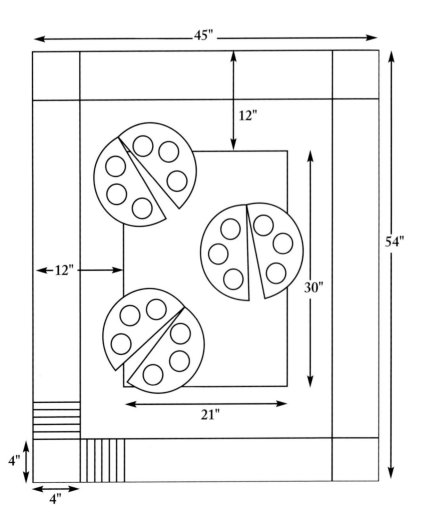

perfect petals

(page 20)

You'll need:
Fleece:
  1 yd. magenta
  ⅓ yd. magenta plaid
  ¼ yd. orange
¼ yd. Steam-A-Seam 2®, 18" wide
Needle and thread
Pinking shears
Pressing cloth

Finished size: 33" x 53"

1. Cut the solid magenta fleece 33" x 53". Use pinking shears to trim the edge of the throw, rounding the corners.

2. Use the pattern on page 61 to cut five flowers from the plaid fleece and use the circle pattern (also on page 61) to cut five circles of Steam-A-Seam 2®. Use the patterns on this page and pinking shears to cut five orange flowers and five magenta circles.

3. Cut five strips of orange ¼" x 10" on the stretchy side of the fabric (see page 3). Curl the strips by holding one end and pulling the other end tightly.

4. Apply the circles of Steam-A-Seam 2® to the backs of the large flowers and iron them to the throw in a random pattern (using a pressing cloth). Check to be sure they're ironed on securely. If not, press again.

5. To complete each flower, place an orange flower centered on the large flower and then the magenta circle centered on that. Pin the curly tie in the middle and sew through all the layers with a sharp needle and thread.

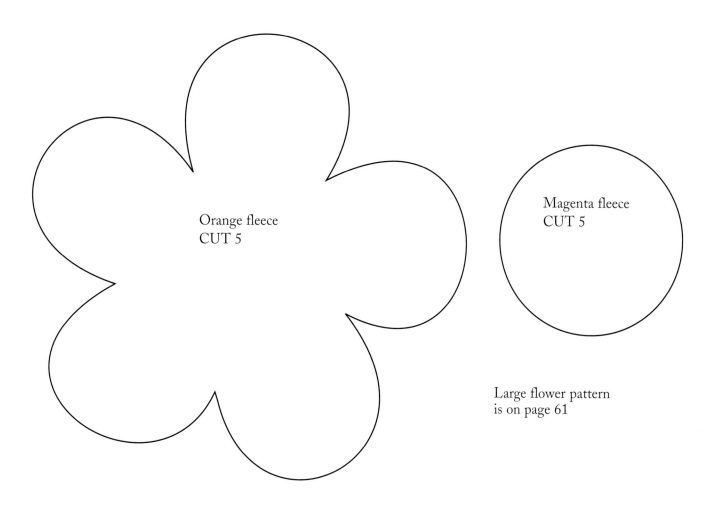

Orange fleece
CUT 5

Magenta fleece
CUT 5

Large flower pattern
is on page 61

it's a tie

(page 22)

You'll need:
Fleece:
  2 yds. navy blue
  Scraps of various primary colors

Finished size: 50" x 60"

1. Cut the blue fleece 50" x 60".

2. Cut 38 ties 1" x 10". Use a variety of colors.

3. On one side, fold the edge up 8 ½" and pin to hold. Starting 11" in from the side, cut 1" slits along the fold every 2"(see diagram). Repeat on the three remaining sides.

4. Thread a tie through two adjoining slits and tie in a knot (A). Continue all around the throw, threading and knotting, alternating the colors of the ties.

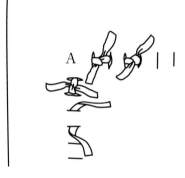

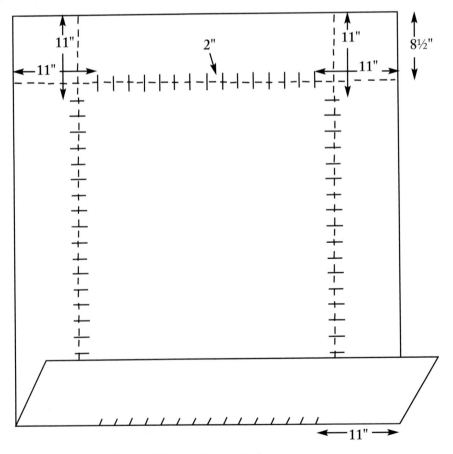

Dashed lines indicate folds

starry, starry night

(page 24)

You'll need:

Fleece:
   1⅓ yds. blue-and-white plaid
   1 yd. star print
Yarn, scraps of assorted colors
Needle and thread
3½ yds. Steam-A-Seam 2®
   fusing tape, ½" wide
½ yd. Steam-A-Seam 2®, 18" wide
Pressing cloth

Finished size: 46" x 56"

1. Cut the plaid fabric 46" x 56". Cut the star print 20" x 26".

2. Apply strips of fusing tape around the edges of the 20" x 26" star piece.

Peel off the backing paper, turn the star piece over and center it on the throw. Place a pressing cloth over the fleece, then iron it on to the throw.

3. With the remaining star fabric, apply a large piece of Steam-A-Seam 2®. Cut out several stars of varying sizes and colors (about 20).

4. Cut the scraps of yarn into 7" pieces (enough to sew to each cut-out star). Tie each in a knot. Sew the yarn tie securely to the stars using a needle and thread.

5. Peel off the backing paper, then iron the stars randomly around the throw using a pressing cloth.

6. Cut ½" x 3" fringe all around the edge of the throw.

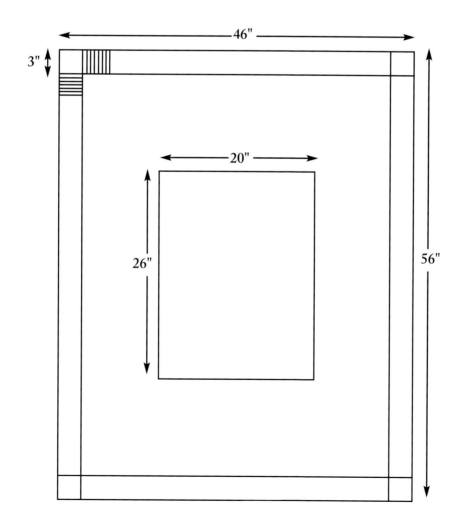

over the rainbow

(page 26)

You'll need:

Fleece:

1½ yds. pastel rainbow print

8 yds. Steam-A-Seam 2® fusing tape, ½" wide

Needle and thread

Pressing cloth

Finished size: 40" x 48"

1. Cut the fleece 40" x 48".

2. Cut out twelve 6" squares from various parts of the rainbow fleece to get an assortment of colors.

3. Apply strips of fusing tape around the edges of the squares. Peel off the backing paper, turn the squares over and using a pressing cloth, iron them to the throw following the diagram below.

4. Cut out twelve ½" x 2½" strips. Tie them in knots and tack to the center of each square using a needle and thread.

5. Cut ½" x 3" fringe all around the edge of the throw.

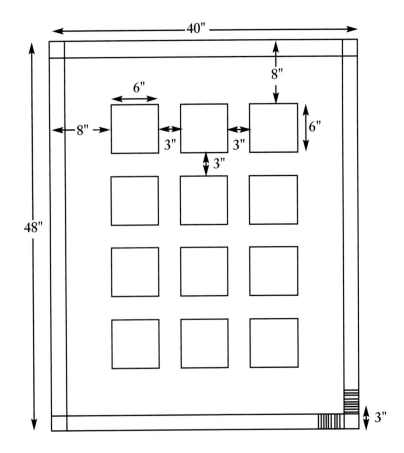

diamonds are forever

(page 28)

You'll need:

Fleece:

   1¼ yds. periwinkle

   ⅓ yd. each pink, lavender, pale yellow and pale green

10 yds. Steam-A-Seam 2® fusing tape, ½" wide

Pressing cloth

Finished size: 42" x 57"

1. Cut the periwinkle fleece 42" x 57".

2. Cut ten 8" squares of the pastel fleece (3 each green and yellow, 2 each pink and lavender).

3. Apply the fusing tape around the edges of each square. Peel off the backing paper, turn the squares over and apply the squares to the periwinkle fleece following the diagram for placement. Pin them in place. Use a pressing cloth and iron the squares to the throw.

4. Use the pattern on page 62 to trace, then cut the two short edges of the throw in points.

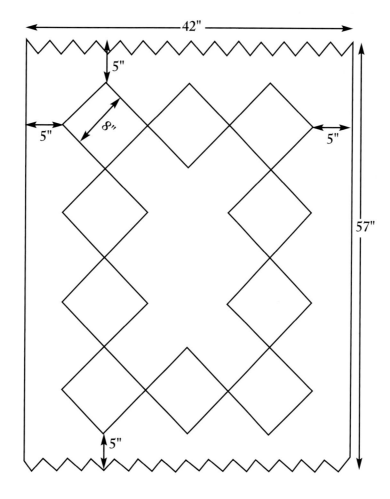

dutch treat

(page 30)

You'll need:

Fleece:
  1¼ yds. periwinkle
  ¾ yd. white
Acrylic paint: Blue Lagoon, Delta
  Ceramcoat
Foam stamp, Casablanca #53626,
  Plaid Ent.
Wide flat brush
8 yds. Steam-A-Seam 2® fusing
  tape, ½" wide
Pressing cloth

Finished size: 40" x 56"

1. Cut blue fleece 40" x 56".

2. Use the patterns on page 62 and page 63 to cut the scallops around the edge of the throw.

3. Cut the white fleece into eight 8" squares, using a wavy edge rotary cutter.

4. To stamp the design: thin the paint with a little water. Brush the paint onto the stamp and then center the stamp on the fabric and press. (Hint: Cut a few extra white squares in case you make a mistake.) Reapply paint after each application. Set the squares aside to dry. To heat set the paint, use the iron with a pressing cloth over the top of the fleece. Or as an alternative, use a heat gun or a blow dryer. If using a heat gun, test it first on the fleece to make sure that it doesn't damage the fabric.

5. Apply fusing tape around the edges of the squares. Peel off the backing paper and apply the squares to the throw (refer to diagram for placement). Use a pressing cloth to iron the squares onto the throw.

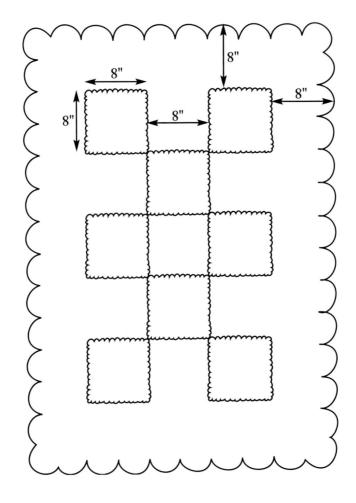

sleeping beauty

(page 32)

You'll need:

Fleece:
  1⅓ yds. sage green
  ⅓ yd. pale green
  ⅛ yd. Steam-A-Seam 2® fusing tape, ½" wide

Finished size: 45" x 56"

1. Cut the green fleece 45" x 56".

2. Cut two strips of pale green 2" x 32" and two strips 2" x 42".

3. To cut slits in the throw for weaving, fold one edge up 6" and pin. Come in 8½" from the end to make the first cut. Refer to the diagram. Cut 1" slits on the fold. Continue to cut slits around the throw every 2" following the diagram for placement.

4. Starting with one short end, thread one 32" strip through the slits coming up from the wrong side. Leave a 1½" tail on the back to secure the strip in place (A). Pin.

5. Continue weaving through the slits until you reach the end. Leave a 1½" tail on the back and pin in place.

6. Continue weaving around the other short end using the 32" strip for the end and then 42" strips for the sides.

7. Cut eight pieces of fusing tape 2" long. Position under each end strip on the back and press (using a pressing cloth) to hold in place.

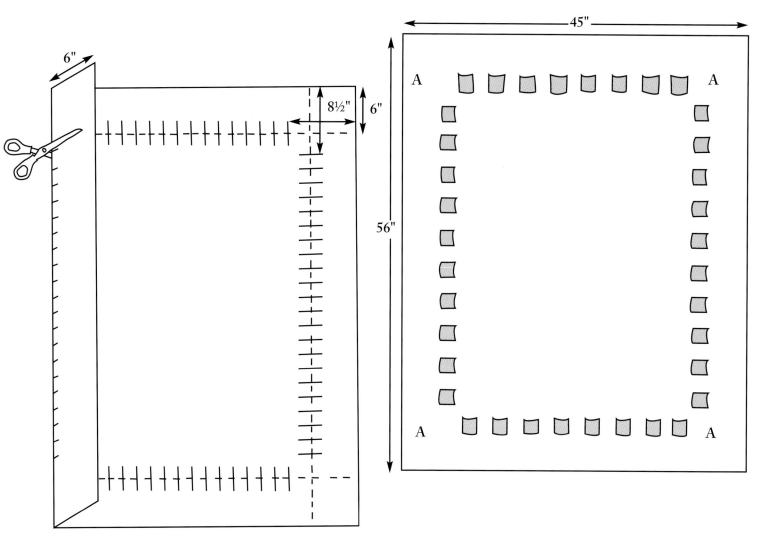

Dashed lines indicate folds

windows

(page 34)

You'll need:

Fleece:
  1½ yds. black
  12" squares of purple, royal blue, green and burgundy
6 yds. Steam-A-Seam 2® fusing tape, ½" wide
Pressing cloth

Finished size: 44" x 54"

1. Cut the black fleece 44" x 54".

2. Cut one each of the four other colors into 12" squares. Fold each square in half. Make a 4" cut where indicated on the diagram (A).

A

3. Fold the square in the opposite direction and make a second 4" cut (B&C).

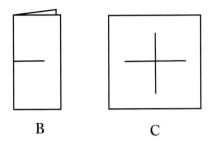

B   C

4. Lay the black fleece on a flat surface.

5. Apply fusing tape around the edge of the squares. Peel off the backing paper and place the squares on the black fleece following the diagram. Use a pressing cloth and iron the squares to the black fleece.

6. Fold back the flaps in the center of the squares (refer to diagram) and pin in place (D).

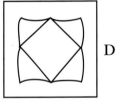

D

7. Cut small squares of fusing tape and place under the tip of each flap and press.

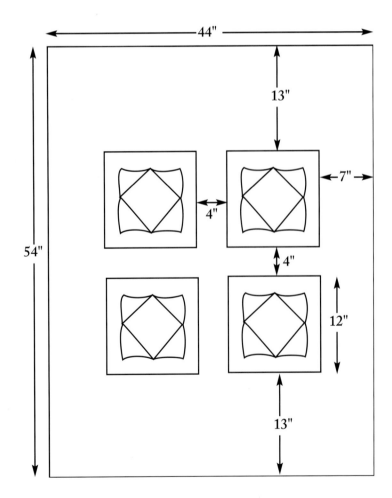

tranquility

(page 36)

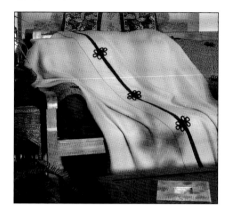

You'll need:

Fleece:
  1½ yds. camel
  1¼ yds. black
3 black frogs
6 yds. Steam-A-Seam 2®
  fusing tape, ½" wide

Finished size: 47" x 58"

1. Cut two pieces of the camel fleece 23" x 58".

2. Cut a black piece 6" x 58".

3. Fold back the two long edges of the camel fleece 3". Apply fusing tape along these edges and iron the fold down (using a pressing cloth).

4. Apply fusing tape on the long edges of the black piece. Peel off the backing paper and place the two camel pieces over the black piece with about 1" of the black showing (A).

5. Using a pressing cloth, iron the camel pieces to the black piece.

6. Tack the three frogs every 10" over the folds (refer to photo for placement).

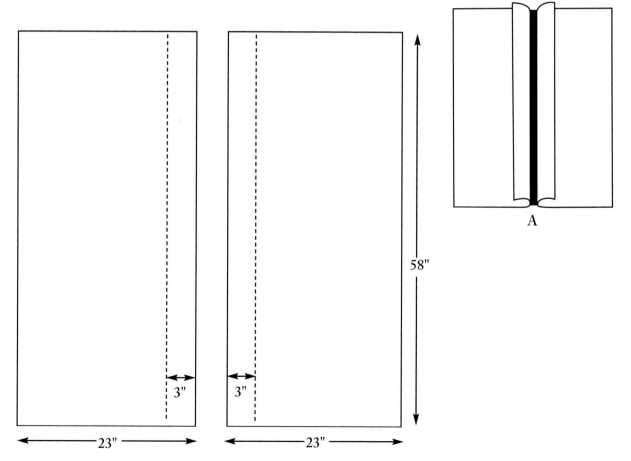

Dashed lines indicate folds

cut to be tied

page 38

You'll need:
Fleece:
  1½ yds. green
  1½ yds. lavender
6 yds. Steam-A-Seam 2® fusing tape,
  ½" wide
Pressing cloth

Finished size: 46" x 54"

1. Cut the green and lavender fleece each 46" x 54".

2. To form the border, fold and cut 2" slits in the green fleece every 1/4" following the diagram below.

3. For the ties: Cut 90 strips of green fleece ¼" x 2".

4. Using a 2" strip, tie six of the border strips together. See diagram (A). Continue around the entire border tying the strips.

5. Apply the fusing tape around the edges of the green fleece. Peel off the backing paper. Position the green fleece on the lavender, matching edges so that the lavender fleece shows through the openings in the green fleece.

6. Using a pressing cloth, iron the two pieces of fleece together.

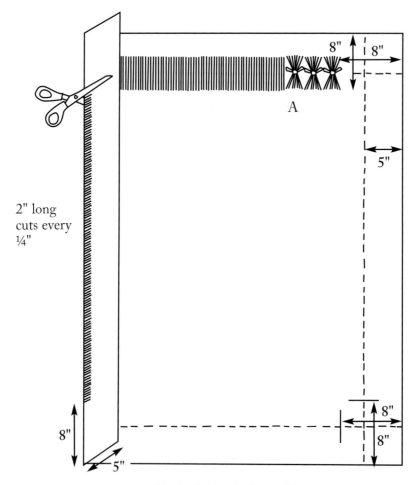

2" long cuts every ¼"

8"

5"

8"

5"

8"

8"

8"

8"

A

Dashed lines indicate folds

primary colors

(page 40)

You'll need:
Fleece:
  1⅓ yds. black
  ⅛ yd. each magenta, lime green,
  orange, blue, red, turquoise, yellow
  and purple
1 yd. Steam-A-Seam 2® fusing tape,
  ½" wide
Pressing cloth
Chacopel pencil

Finished size: 44" x 60"

1. Cut the black fleece 44" x 60".

2. Cut one each of the turquoise, yellow, and purple fleece into 1" x 60" strips. Cut two each of the magenta, lime green, orange, blue and red 1" x 44".

3. To cut slits for weaving: Refer to the diagram (A) Each dashed line represents a fold line. Measure and turn the fabric up to each fold line, and mark the position of the slits using a Chacopel pencil. Clip before continuing to the next fold. Cut ½" slits on the fold (B).

Hint: Complete all the vertical folds before starting the horizontal folds.

4. Weave the color strips. After weaving is complete, iron all of the ends on the back of the throw to secure them using the fusing tape.

5. If desired, apply fusing tape to the backs of the strips on the top part of the throw and iron to secure.

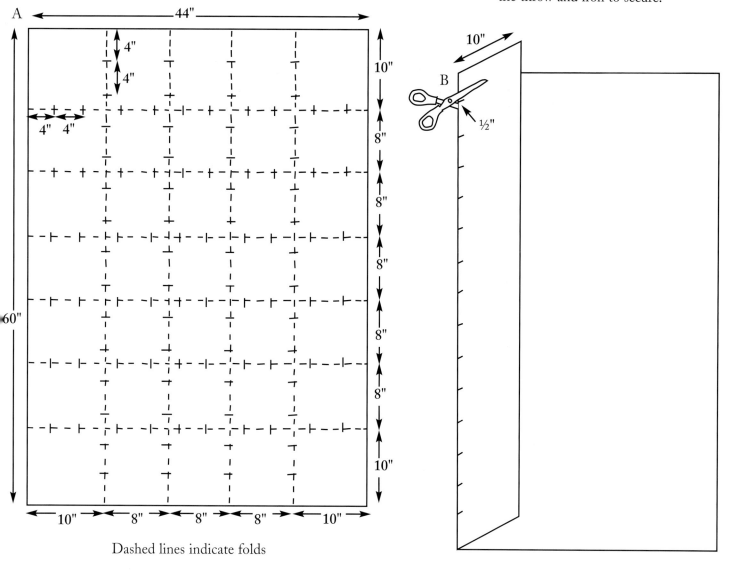

Dashed lines indicate folds

dream weaver

(page 42)

You'll need:

Fleece:
  1½ yds. pink
  1¼ yds. lime green
  1 yd. turquoise
2¼ yds. Craft Fuse™, Pellon®

Finished size: 48" x 56"

1. Cut the pink fleece 48" x 56".

2. Cut four turquoise strips 8" x 56" and five green strips 8" x 48".

3. Lay the four turquoise strips on a large table, butting up to each other, even on both ends.

4. Lay the five green strips over the top of these with 8" extending on all sides, and the green strips butting up to each other.

5. Weave the green strips through the blue strips.

6. Cut a piece of Craft Fuse 32" x 40". Since this comes only 16" wide, you'll have to piece it together to form this size piece. Place the shiny, adhesive side of Craft Fuse against the wrong side of the fabric. Use a pressing cloth, and a hot, dry iron, a gliding motion, and slight pressure to fuse it to the fabric.

7. Position the pink fleece on the woven fleece with wrong sides together and edges matching.

8. Cut 1" x 8" fringe around the throw. Tie the pink backing to the top with the fringe strips in double knots.

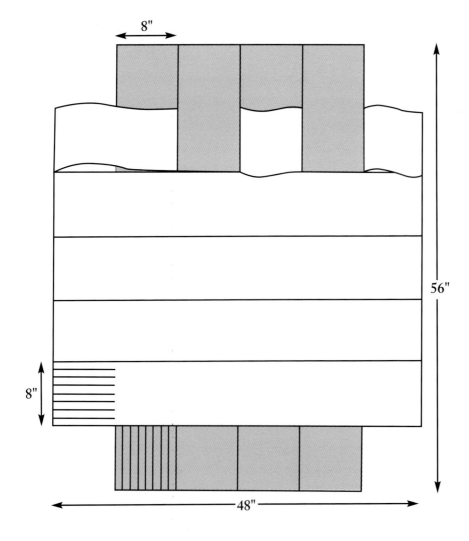

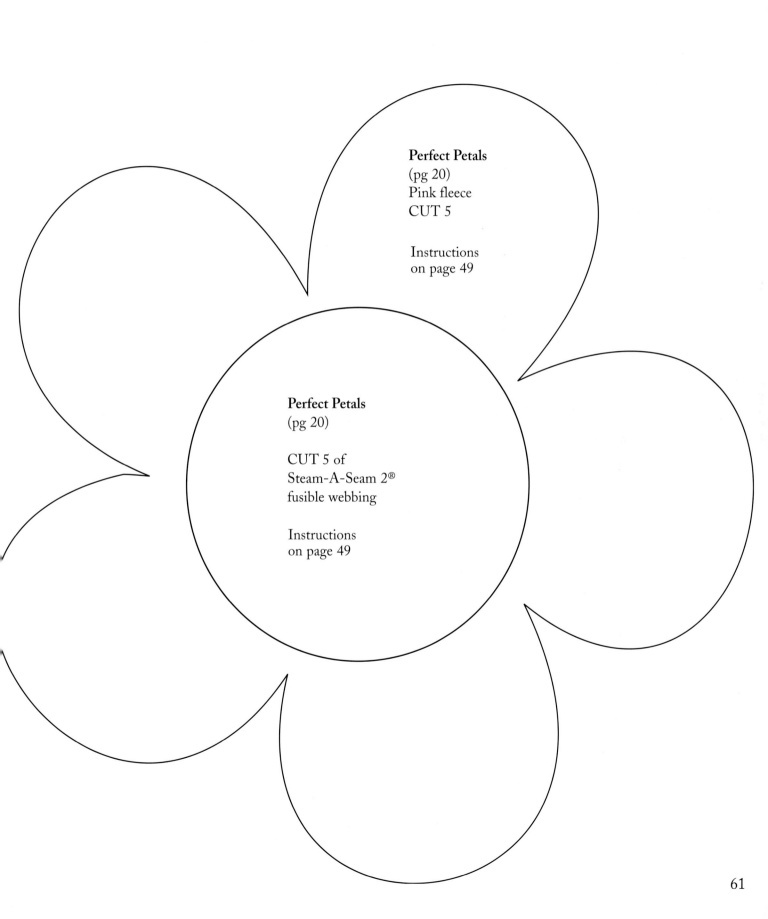

Perfect Petals
(pg 20)
Pink fleece
CUT 5

Instructions
on page 49

Perfect Petals
(pg 20)

CUT 5 of
Steam-A-Seam 2®
fusible webbing

Instructions
on page 49

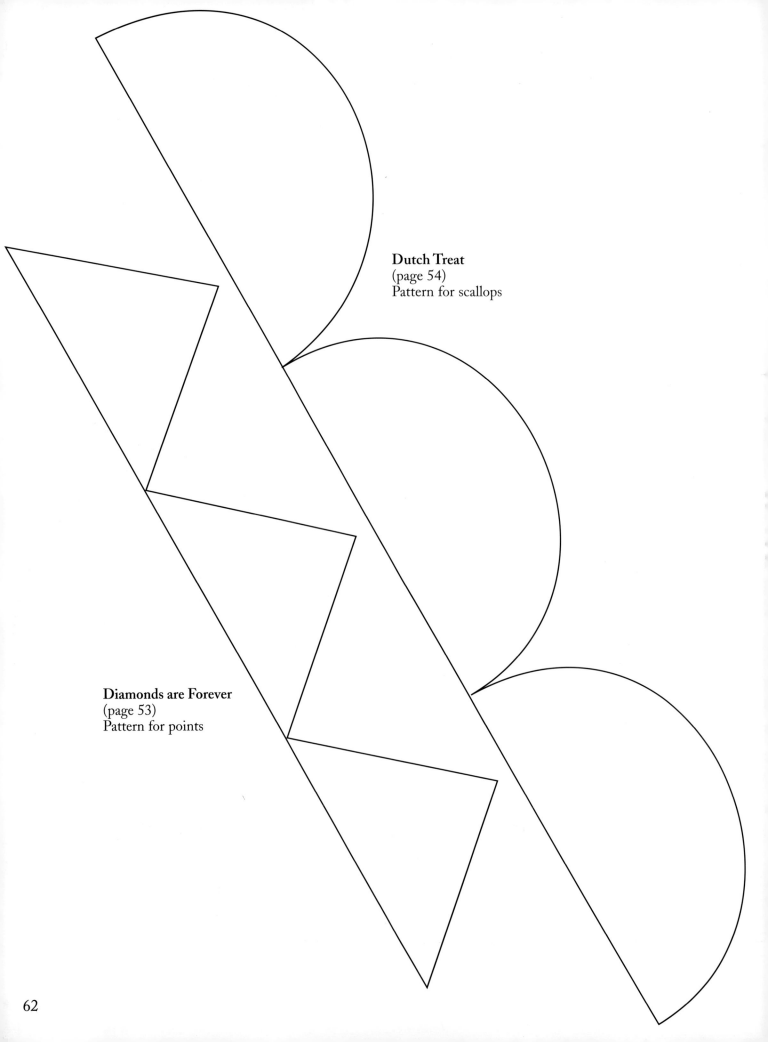

Dutch Treat
(page 54)
Pattern for scallops

Diamonds are Forever
(page 53)
Pattern for points

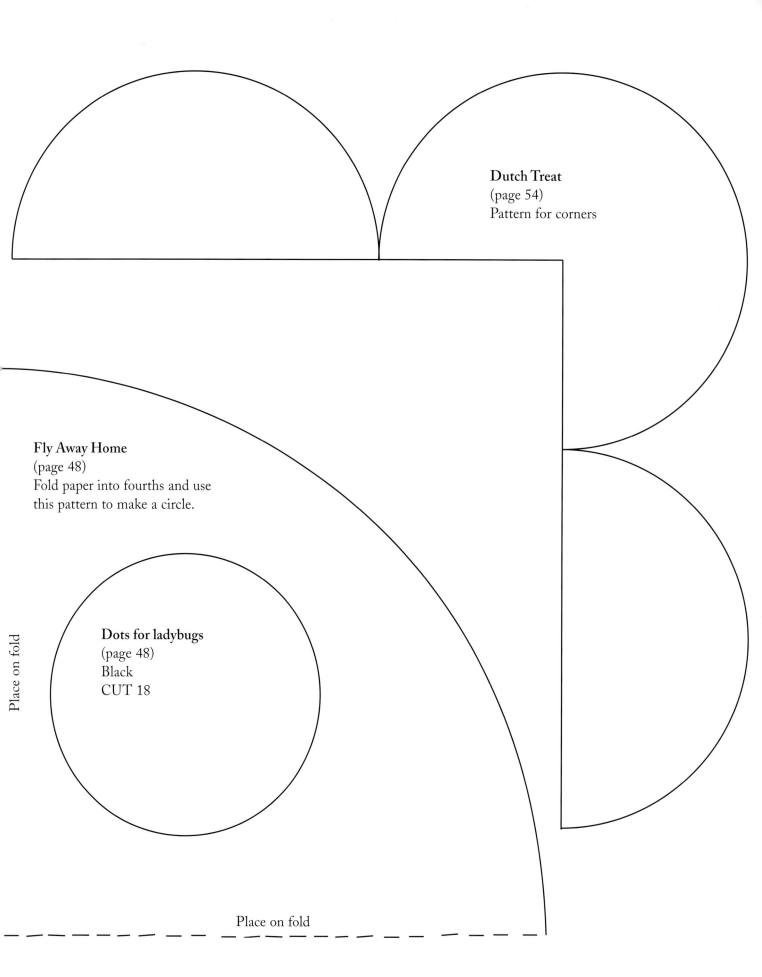

Dutch Treat
(page 54)
Pattern for corners

Fly Away Home
(page 48)
Fold paper into fourths and use
this pattern to make a circle.

Place on fold

Dots for ladybugs
(page 48)
Black
CUT 18

Place on fold

Sources & Credits

Most of the supplies used in this book can be found in your local fabric store. If you can't find the item you're looking for, consult the following companies to find out where their products are sold:

Steam-A-Seam 2®
Fusing tapes and fusible web
The Warm Company
954 E. Union Street
Seattle, WA 98122
www.warmcompany.com

Craft Fuse™
Pellon®
Freudenberg Nonwovens
3440 Industrial Dr.
Durham, NC 27704

Acrylic Paint
Delta Technical Coatings
2550 Pellissier Pl.
Whittier, CA 90601
www.deltacrafts.com

Chacopel Pencils
Clover
1007 E. Dominguez St.
Carson, CA 90746
(310) 516-7846

Foam Stamps
Plaid Enterprises
3225 Westech Dr.
Norcross, GA 30092
www.plaidonline.com

Foam Beads
Creative Hands
Fibre-Craft Materials Corp.
Niles, IL 60714
www.creativehands.net

We'd like to thank our teen apprentices Dana Whalen, Kelly Conners and Loren Johnson for their invaluable help with this book.

Banar Designs Principals:
Barbara Finwall and Nancy Javier
Art Direction: Barbara Finwall
Editorial Direction: Nancy Javier

Photography: Stephen Whalen
Computer Graphic Design: Mark Aron
Project Direction: Jerilyn Clements
Designs by: Nancy Javier, Jerilyn Clements,
  Barbara Finwall

Published by

LEISURE ARTS
5701 Ranch Drive
Little Rock, AR 72223
© 2004 by Leisure Arts, Inc.

Produced by

BANAR DESIGNS

P.O. Box 483
Fallbrook, CA 92088
banar@adelphia.net

The information in this publication is presented in good faith, but no warranty is given, nor results guaranteed. Since we have no control over physical conditions surrounding the application of information herein contained, Leisure Arts, Inc. disclaims any liability for untoward results.